BLOODSUCKING LAMPREYS

By Ryan Nagelhout

Gareth Stevens
PUBLISHING

Please visit our website, www.garethstevens.com. For a free color catalog of all our high-quality books, call toll free 1-800-542-2595 or fax 1-877-542-2596.

Cataloging-in-Publication Data

Nagelhout, Ryan.
Bloodsucking lampreys / by Ryan Nagelhout.
p. cm. — (Real-life vampires)
Includes index.
ISBN 978-1-4824-3947-2 (pbk.)
ISBN 978-1-4824-3948-9 (6-pack)
ISBN 978-1-4824-3949-6 (library binding)
1. Bloodsucking animals — Juvenile literature. 2. Cold-blooded animals — Juvenile literature. I. Nagelhout, Ryan. II. Title.
QL756.55 N34 2016
591.53—d23

First Edition

Published in 2016 by
Gareth Stevens Publishing
111 East 14th Street, Suite 349
New York, NY 10003

Designer: Katelyn E. Reynolds
Editor: Kristen Nelson

Photo credits: Cover, pp. 1, 17 James L. Amos/National Geographic/Getty Images; cover, pp. 1–24 (background art) happykanppy/Shutterstock.com; pp. 5, 11 (inset) DeAgostini/Getty Images; p. 7 (main) MIGUEL RIOPA/AFP/Getty Images; p. 7 (inset) Reinhard Dirscherl/ullstein bild via Getty Images; p. 9 Wil Meinderts/Buiten-beeld/Minden Pictures/Getty Images; p. 11 (main) Jonathan Bird/Photolibrary/Getty Images; p. 13 George Skadding/The LIFE Picture Collection/Getty Images; p. 15 (map) Rainer Lesniewski/Shutterstock.com; p. 15 (inset) Gzuckier/Wikimedia Commons; p. 19 Rebaschus/ullstein bild via Getty Images; p. 21 (lamprey illustration) Morphart Creation/Shutterstock.com.

Printed in the United States of America

CPSIA compliance information: Batch #CW16GS: For further information contact Gareth Stevens, New York, New York at 1-800-542-2595.

CONTENTS

Words in the glossary appear in **bold** type
the first time they are used in the text.

IT'S RAINING TEETH!

In 2015, people living in Fairbanks, Alaska, noticed something strange falling from the sky. Tubelike fish with round rows of sharp teeth were found in parking lots and on front lawns all over town. These freaky creatures were Arctic lampreys, bloodsucking fish that use their teeth to hold on to their **prey**.

The lampreys were probably dropped by gulls flying overhead, giving people a good look at these scary animals out of the water. Let's find out more about these real-life **vampires**!

Lampreys look like slimy snakes.
Their gills are used to breathe in the water.

gills

OLD FISH

Lampreys are a member of the animal group Agnatha. They've lived on Earth for more than 400 million years. There are more than 40 different lamprey species. Most lampreys live along seacoasts and in freshwater in **temperate** areas, but some—such as Arctic lampreys—live in colder waters.

Lampreys range in size from 6 to 40 inches (15 to 100 cm) long. They're often called eels, but the two are very different. Eels have bones, while lamprey bodies are made of **cartilage**.

FACT BITE

The easiest way to tell the difference between an eel and a lamprey is to look at their mouths! Eels are also larger than lampreys at about 4 pounds (1.8 kg) and up to 5 feet (1.5 m) long.

lamprey

eel

THIRST FOR BLOOD

A lamprey's mouth might make it just as scary as any vampire story! It's open and disc-shaped with rows of sharp teeth.

Lampreys are **parasites** that feed on the blood and body fluids of fish. Their mouth works like a **suction cup**, and their hornlike teeth dig into the side of the fish's body. Lampreys use their bumpy tongue to clear away fish scales and skin, then they make a hole to suck blood from. It's hard to remove a lamprey when it's feeding.

As a member of Agnatha, lampreys are **jawless** fish. That's clear when you see their frightening mouth up close—they don't look like other fish's mouths!

STOP THE CLOT

Lampreys create an **enzyme** in their mouth that keeps their prey's blood from clotting, or thickening. Lampreys can get lots of blood out of a fish! However, that doesn't mean they always kill the fish they feed from.

Fish that **evolved** alongside lampreys have learned to deal with attacks by their local vampires. Those that survive a lamprey attack have round marks from the lamprey on their body. Weaker fish—especially those not used to living with lampreys—can die from a lamprey bite, though.

FACT BITE

sea lamprey

brook lamprey

LAMPREY LIFE CYCLE

Sea lampreys live about 5 to 9 years. Adult sea lampreys swim into freshwater rivers and streams to spawn, or come together to produce babies from eggs. They build a nest by moving stones with their mouths to make a shallow, sandy hole. Once they've laid the eggs there, lamprey parents will die.

After lamprey eggs **hatch**, the larvae dig into mud in the riverbed or streambed. Sea lampreys live there for 3 to 5 years eating tiny creatures that live in the water.

FACT BITE

13

FRESHWATER START

When sea lampreys grow 4 to 5 inches (10 to 12 cm) long, they leave the muddy river bottom and become adults. Sea lampreys travel back to their usual saltwater **habitat**. When lampreys are ready to spawn, they return to the same river or stream where they once hatched!

Many sea lampreys live in freshwater all their life. They're called an invasive species because they're not living in their normal habitat and cause problems for native fish.

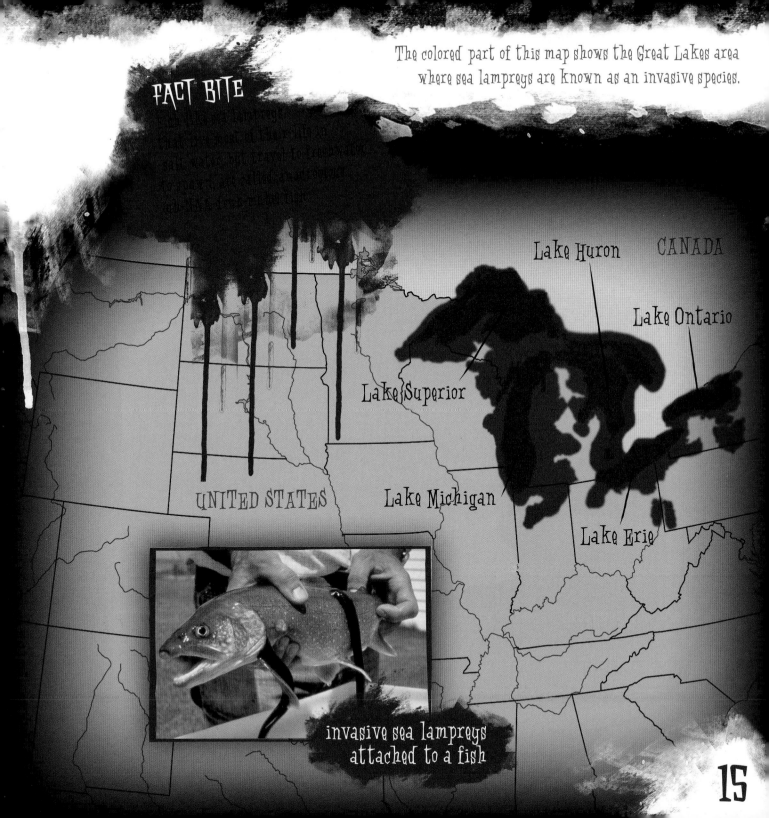

FACT BITE

Lake Huron   CANADA

Lake Ontario

Lake Superior

UNITED STATES

Lake Michigan

Lake Erie

invasive sea lampreys
attached to a fish

15

KILLING BUSINESS

Sea lampreys entered the Great Lakes during the 1800s and early 1900s. The lakes offered good spawning grounds, lots of fish to feed on, and very few predators. Lampreys spread quickly!

Sea lampreys aren't just vampires—they're business killers! Most Great Lakes fish can't survive a lamprey attack, or they die from an **infected** wound made by a lamprey's bite. Because of this, lampreys nearly wiped out parts of the fishing industry in the Great Lakes in the 1960s.

In the 1960s, about 85 percent of fish caught by commercial fisheries in the Great Lakes showed marks of a lamprey attack.

VAMPIRE CONTROL

The United States and Canadian governments have worked to control the sea lamprey population in the Great Lakes to keep other wildlife safe. Fishermen are asked to kill lampreys they find stuck to fish and not to throw lampreys back into the water.

In some places, special barriers, or walls, are put into the water that don't allow lampreys through. Native fish are able to get through these, but lampreys are trapped and stopped from moving upstream to spawn.

FACT BITE

Some places use lampricide,
a special poison that kills
lamprey larvae but doesn't harm
people, plants, and most fish.

If allowed to spawn in the Great Lakes,
a sea lamprey may lay 100,000 eggs!

FISH FOOD?

Lampreys may look scary, but it's good to remember these bloodsucking fish are much more harmful to other fish than they are to people. Not all lampreys are parasites, either. Some freshwater lampreys are native to the Great Lakes, and they don't harm fish.

Some people even like to eat lampreys. Thousands of years ago, Romans caught lampreys and put them in pies and pudding! Would you chow down on these vampire fish?

FACT BITE

Sea lampreys found in freshwater may not be native to it. They are often thought of as invasive likely because of their damage to the populations of native fish, such as trout.

SEA LAMPREY LIFE CYCLE

Adult lampreys go to freshwater to spawn.

Lampreys lay eggs.

Lampreys suck fish blood for 12 to 18 months.

Larvae hatch.

Adult lampreys swim to sea.

Larvae dig into the mud and grow.

Sea lampreys have a special part of their life cycle when they have to feed on blood!

GLOSSARY

cartilage: the bendable matter that makes up your ears and nose, and takes the place of bones in some fish

enzyme: matter made in the body that helps certain actions necessary for life to occur

evolve: to grow and change over time

habitat: the natural place where an animal or plant lives

hatch: to come out of

infected: filled with germs

jawless: not having jaws, or the walls of the mouth

parasite: a living thing that lives in, on, or with another living thing and often harms it

prey: an animal hunted by other animals for food

suction cup: a round cup that is fixed to a surface when pressed against it

temperate: mild weather that's not too hot or too cold

vampire: a made-up being who drinks human blood

FOR MORE INFORMATION

Books

May, Suellen. *Invasive Aquatic and Wetland Animals.* New York, NY: Chelsea House, 2007.

Somervill, Barbara A. *Sea Lamprey.* Ann Arbor, MI: Cherry Lake Publishing, 2008.

Websites

Arctic Lamprey
www.adfg.alaska.gov/index.cfm?adfg=arcticlamprey.main
Find out more about the Arctic lamprey and how it lives in cold waters.

Bloodsucking Lampreys
www.animalplanet.com/tv-shows/river-monsters/videos/a-kiss-of-death-lamprey-sucks-jeremys-blood/
This scary video shows what happens when a lamprey attaches itself to a person's neck!

Sea Lamprey
glfc.org/sealamp
Learn more about how sea lampreys hurt Great Lakes fish here.

INDEX